PHOTOGRAPHERS' BRITAIN

PHOTOGRAPHERS' BRITAIN

DORSET

To
Callie my wife
and my daughter
Charlotte
Born on Mother's Day

PHOTOGRAPHERS' BRITAIN

DORSET

TIM HAWKINS

ALAN SUTTON

First published in the United Kingdom in 1991
Alan Sutton Publishing Ltd · Phoenix Mill · Far Thrupp · Stroud · Gloucestershire

---

First published in the United States of America in 1991
Alan Sutton Publishing Inc · Wolfeboro Falls · NH 03896-0848

British Library Cataloguing in Publication Data

Hawkins, Tim
Photographers' Britain, Dorset.
1. England. Photography
I. Title
779.994233

Cased ISBN 0 86299 985 5
Paperback ISBN 0 86299 841 7

Library of Congress Cataloging-in-Publication Data

Hawkins, Tim.
Dorset / Tim Hawkins.
p. cm.
ISBN 0–86299–841–7: $19.00
1. Dorset (England) – Description and travel – Views. I. Title.
DA670.D7H38 1991
914.23'3–dc20 91–3469
CIP

Title page photograph: Coney's Castle to Charmouth

Cover photograph: St Alban's Head

Typeset in Sabon 10/14
Typesetting and origination by
Alan Sutton Publishing Limited.
Printed in Great Britain by
The Bath Press, Avon.

ACKNOWLEDGEMENTS

Indulging in landscape photography is generally a very solitary occupation, but I have received help and constructive criticism from many quarters. In particular I would like to thank John Lewis, Adrian King and Rob Ormsby for being so hospitable. Laurence Keen, the County Archaeological Officer, Reg Parry, Steve Wilson and Ruth Philips all helped to correct or provide me with additional information. Leo Gough made me put into words my *modus operandi* after having been dragged around Dorset. Tim Page's advice and criticism has kept me on the tracks. Besides Colin and Jenny Glanfield; Wayne Clark, Millie Dolan, Gill Ward, Rob Fuke and Don Hughes have all been greatly amused by my first drafts and have helped me turn them into second and third ones.

Without Roby Littman I would never have known Dorset. Also thanks to Colette Littman who has helped in many ways. I would like to thank both Peter Clifford and Jaqueline Mitchell for their patience; my mother for her astute criticism and encouragement, and my wife, Callie for her all round support and understanding especially when I would suddenly disappear into the expanse of Dorset at the whim of a weather forecast.

INTRODUCTION

Having had a nomadic upbringing, the only thing my birth entitles me to do is to play cricket for Yorkshire. I turned up in an army barracks: it happened to be Pontefract. No, I don't like the cakes. The question of where I was born had little relevance. Therefore, until my early teens, I was county-less. It was then that a school friend invited me to stay with his parents in Gaunt's Common, which happened to be in Dorset. All I knew of Dorset at that time was that it had rather special geological features and was a favourite topic of my geography teacher. I could draw a sketch of the formation of Lulworth Cove at the slightest provocation. Shortly afterwards I was able to see these features 'in the flesh', they being described to me as 'Dorset Spectaculars'. I readily agreed with these sentiments and from that time on Dorset became my visual playground.

I have exercised my camera on the landscape of Dorset more than any other location. Its diversity of physical character provides a marvellous complement to the vagaries of the British weather. My earliest attempts at photography in Dorset were all in black and white, because I couldn't afford colour film. I also couldn't afford particularly brilliant lenses, resulting in many of these earlier negatives being banished to the back of the shelf. Now, I am back to where I started, and this time by choice: I feel that the Dorset landscape can be far better expressed without colour. I enjoy the greater freedom of expression and flexibility of black and white film. I do have to say, however, that there is always the exception to the rule, and in many of my commissions colour is essential.

Throughout the book I refer to the quality of light. To make the greatest use of the ambient light, I try to understand and interpret the British weather. Such a task is not easy, as by the time the forecasts have filtered down through various channels, discrepancies start to appear. This is incredibly frustrating, as light, and the way that the landscape reacts to it, rules my photography. Therefore, on certain high points throughout Dorset I have weather watching spots, where I retreat to reassess the situation when the forecasts are wrong.

I have not concentrated on the architecture and buildings of Dorset. Unusually for me, I have only included them when they have become an integral part of the landscape, as in the case of the lighthouses on Portland Bill. I have also allowed one photograph of urban Dorset to sneak in; Weymouth harbour at night. Most are familiar with Corfe Castle, and even I could not resist the temptation to take a picture, but in the main I wanted to show the lesser known parts of the county. Certainly, there are views such as that from Abbotsbury Hill which are almost clichéd, but being one of the first 'Spectaculars' I saw, it's inclusion was guaranteed. I make no apologies for having two shots of Durdle Door.

I feel a strong photographic attachment to the edifices of the ancient inhabitants of Dorset. These have had a direct influence on the shape of the landscape, especially on the upland areas. The chalk hills in the past provided a comparative haven overlooking the wooded lowland areas. Around Nettlecombe Tout, for instance, there is hardly a field that doesn't contain some type of feature from the pre-Roman era. Of the many hill forts from Penbury Knoll (on the Hampshire border), to Lambert's Castle (north of Lyme Regis), Eggardon Hill is to me, the most impressive and photogenic.

The impact of the twentieth century on Dorset has been immense. Authors from each decade have written about the 'unknown' aspects of the county, but sadly these are becoming fewer and less 'lost' each year. Increased tourism, better communications and outward pressure from the south-east have ensured this. I have touched on the disintegration of the open heathlands, a depressing state of affairs, but much of rural Dorset is still exceptionally beautiful; a visit to Marshwood Vale will confirm this. It would be easy to portray a gloomy picture of present-day Dorset, but I am an optimist.

People often say that photography beats working and I have to admit that rambling around Dorset, taking these pictures, has been a delightful enterprise to undertake. In compiling this book, I have driven down nearly every country lane in Dorset, and have been subjected to everything that the glorious British climate could throw at me. This last was rather under-estimated by my geography textbook!

BESIDE STAIR HOLE

Mupe Rocks and Portland

Much of Flowers Barrow Fort has disappeared into the sea; the Iron Age earthworks are now oddly truncated, hanging in limbo some 500 feet above the bay. I first visited the end of this chalk escarpment several years ago to take a midwinter shot of the sunrise filling Mupe Bay. The light was fabulous. On that occasion it was bitterly cold when I arrived well before dawn, as the strong wind was making the 5 degrees of frost extremely penetrating. Weighed down by a complete overkill of photographic gear, including a 5 × 4 plate camera, I almost lost all feeling in my extremities in the biting air. The $1\frac{1}{2}$ mile walk from the car made me thoroughly determined to get a good shot. Despite the tripod being buffeted by the wind I came away with two successful frames of this view. Unfortunately they only work in colour.

My personal pilgrimage brought me back to the same point to retake the shot, but this time in black and white. I had waited for a day with a north-westerly wind, hoping that the clouds would tend to break up over the coast. This happened, and, combined with the *contre-jour* effect, made the photograph totally different from the previous dawn shot. This is one of the most remarkable places in Dorset, for looking around from this half-eroded fort the unique landscape of the county becomes clear. It therefore seems apt to enclose the photographs in the book between the two taken from this exact point.

Derrick on Portland Bill

Watching waves relentlessly crashing onto solid rock is a very satisfying experience and in the final moments of their brief lives each wave has its own unique character. At the height of severe Channel storms it is impossible to take any photographs whilst on the Bill, as even in the car-park the horizontal salt spray keeps all but the intrepid inside their steamed up vehicles; salt also kills cameras. The previous February night the Bill had been blasted by a force 10 storm, not that severe. However in the lee of the Bill the sea had a different appearance, less ragged, and the waves appeared more controlled as they ponderously dumped their tons of water on the already glistening rocks of the raised beach. At this particular location one needs to watch out for spray as the crashing waves compress the air so that moments later spray is belched out many feet into the air. Inevitably the most interesting surf occurs as the tripod is being erected and the cameras are still in the case. However I took six frames over a period of twenty minutes and was left with the impression that the power in the waves was visibly diminishing – time to move on.

Lewesdon Hill and Pilsdon Pen

I distinctly remember taking this picture, and then losing it amongst all the other negatives and forgetting that it even existed. It is rare to forget the circumstances surrounding a particular photograph. On this day the weather forecast had been up the spout and everything was happening about four hours later than expected, which literally put a damper on the occasion.

When the weather is foul, I often drive to where it will break first as the light immediately afterwards can be very interesting – in this case towards the west of the county. Keeping just to the north of the central ridge of hills which continues right across into Devon, I stopped just before Broadwindsor. It was here that Charles Stuart narrowly escaped capture by Cromwell's forces during his flight from England. This approach road luckily has low hedges and to the left I suddenly saw the cloud cover beginning to break; one ray was soon followed by a brief burst of intense sunlight, akin to one of William Blake's visions of the Book of Job. My camera was ready for this glorious spectacle. It was a fortunate place to stop as I was able to use the wood-clad Lewesdon Hill and the Iron Age fortifications on Pilsdon Pen as a backdrop. This was the most rewarding shot of the day; I have rejected the others. An afternoon's photography for a single printable frame.

Nettlecombe Tout

Part of the small plateau between the Dorset Gap and the hamlet of Folly has been cordoned off by a cross dyke enclosing a 15-acre site thought to be an unfinished hill fort. In fact the whole area shows evidence of Celtic agriculture with further dykes and burial mounds. It was once a very busy hill top! Not so today, as one doesn't stumble across this region accidently; even the Fox Inn in the tiny hamlet of Folly has ceased to exist because of lack of patronage. It is a marvellous walk from there, up the ancient paths onto Nettlecombe Tout. I placed the tripod atop the scarp slope on the north side of the plateau overlooking the expanse of the Vale of Blackmoor beneath. The textured cross-light on the trees together with the peculiar conurbation of moss-covered roots, the result of much earlier coppicing activity, drew me to this spot on an early April day.

The Stour near Hammoon

The fact that the Stour breaks through the chalk uplands to the north-west of Blandford is attributable to the last Ice Age, when the Vale of Blackmoor was probably a vast periglacial lake. Later much of it became marshland, and it must have been an inhospitable place to the Stone and Iron Age inhabitants, who mainly resided in the drier uplands such as Hambledon Hill fort, on the horizon, from where they could look upon the vale and any approaching danger. Today, the river rises in Wiltshire and, together with its tributaries, drains the now fertile vale.

Hammoon is one of many small hamlets scattered across this northern part of the county; it lies a hundred yards or so to the south of the Stour, dangerously close should the river flood in winter. I was leaving Dorset to the north not expecting to take any more frames. However crossing the Stour late on this summer's evening I thought that a shot was worth it as I had two frames left on the roll. The second 8-second exposure was the one I chose.

Iwerne from Hambledon Hill

Rising abruptly out of the south-east corner of the Vale of Blackmoor is the fortified chalk spur of Hambledon Hill. Together with Hod Hill further to the south it dominates the exit of the Stour from the vale. There isn't the same feeling of isolation and starkness as at Eggardon Hill (see page 29), so I wanted to treat the area in a different way photographically. Ascending Hambledon Hill from Child Okeford, there was a thick early morning mist making the light very flat but I was enjoying the gentle crumble of the frost underfoot as I hurried up the steepening slope. For me there is always a slight sense of panic when I know that the light and conditions are right and that I'm not in the right place to take advantage of them. The vagaries of interesting photographic light always seem to be so temporary, with little time to collect one's thoughts, and decide on the best course of action. However I managed to reach the east side of Hambledon Hill, where above an Iron Age fortification, overlooking Iwerne, I arrived in time to capture the last remnants of the mist in the valley. I then proceeded on my circuit of the fort thoroughly enjoying the brisk morning.

The Stour at Charlton Marshall

Wires be damned. There are so many occasions when potential shots are nipped in the bud by electrical pylons and cables relentlessly snaking across the landscape. The wires over the Stour in flood at Charlton Marshall were not going to stop me this time in my search for an interesting flooded landscape. Sometimes in summer one scarcely notices Dorset's rivers, their levels reduced behind the thick foliage of overhanging bushes and trees. When the greenery is absent in winter and it pours with rain, the scene can change dramatically. Thankfully obscured in the background behind the church and the trees are what Pevsner describes as 'the culs-de-sacs of bungalows . . . suburbia in rure at its worst'. I suspect that the architect of the church in Charlton Marshall, Thomas Horlock Bastard, who died aged 102, would not have appreciated this modern style of construction in his village.

THE HAVEN FROM SANDBANKS

The Haven forms a natural barrier to the southward encroachment of the towns Poole and Bournemouth. Across the narrow channel is the nature reserve on Studland Heath, part of the Isle of Purbeck. The tide rips through the haven and just beyond the jetty it shelves very steeply. The bottom has been scoured to a depth of 70 feet. However, offshore a few hundred yards into Poole Bay are Hook Sands, which rarely show themselves – the home of many a propellor. Boats that have foundered here are said to be swallowed up by the shifting sands. Occasionally the turrets and barrels of some tanks reappear beneath the water; they were lost during the preparations for D-Day in 1944.

Looking across to the Purbecks, I've wondered whether a national park might one day be created here, including the islands and south shore of Poole harbour. But this would be hampered if the mooted privatization of the harbour takes place. At the present it is run and organized on a non-profit basis. Should this alter, the change in emphasis may ruin this fragile environment before the need to conserve it is clearly understood.

KIMMERIDGE, CLAVELL'S PIER

Only two industries have ever succeeded at Kimmeridge Bay and neither of them were connected with Sir William Clavell. One was based on the Romans' fascination for trinkets made from the local Blackstone, and the other was the extraction of oil from the shale, 1,500 feet down, by means of the camouflaged 'Nodding Donkey'.

Clavell's claim to fame was that he was a born loser; he failed to find the Midas Touch and the remains of this pier is his monument. The year 1745 saw not only the end of the Young Pretender's hopes at Culloden Field, but also the end of Sir William's enormous and absurdly high structure jutting into Kimmeridge Bay, where it was battered to pieces during a storm. He never witnessed this event as he had died in prison some hundred years earlier. I became fascinated by the pier's existence after seeing it in Paul Nash's *A Shell Guide to Dorset* (1935), and the angle of my shot has differed little. The sea-polished blocks of local stone have a reflective quality when wet, and the lengthy exposure gives the water a mystical feel. I equate the storm's destruction of the unnecessary pier with Nash's dedication in his book to 'All Those Enemies of Development To Whom We Owe What Is Left Of England'. Thank goodness Kimmeridge never became a bustling little port.

Chiswell Boats

Few people realize that Chiswell actually exists. The Ordnance Survey term the area 'Chesil' and another older map refers to 'Chesill Tonne'. I am not sure who first gave it its present elusive name, but the now defunct Weymouth & Portland Railway named its first stop on Portland as Chiswell Station. Leaving the island, the road guides one through the heart of the village and the incongruity of a little cluster of boats on a grass verge below the chapel on the right has always amused me. During storms in the late seventies this area suffered severe flooding. The boats are certainly safe now against the ravages of the storms that pound against the Chesil Bank as new sea defences have been built. The buildings today stand in a very similar position to those erected by the Romans – hard against the back slope of the beach. However they would not have recognized the modern day chariot, *Robinimus Relianticus*, nestled against the stone wall.

CHISWELL
WH142
PRINTER

Lighthouses, Portland Bill

Man first left his mark on the low-lying southern end of Portland towards Bill Point in the Stone Age, but traces of this and later pre-Roman settlements have now all but vanished.

The first two lighthouses came into operation in 1716, the lower of which (in the foreground), is now a bird observatory. It became redundant in 1906 when the new 118-foot tower on the Bill itself came into operation. Much of the old common land is now a total mess, submerged under tarmac and cars. But despite this, the feeling of vulnerability pervades. Portland Bill is the southernmost part of Dorset, and the wind and the sea rule this domain. I decided to simplify the shot by exposing for the brighter sky, thus obscuring the distracting foreground. In the distance, beyond the new lighthouse, are the many tidal races and the shoaling sands of the Shambles which combine to make the Bill a treacherous coastline even on a calm day such as this.

Chesil Bank

Before I had even set eyes on this part of the Dorset coastline I knew of this feature, and its description ensured a few extra marks in my geography exam. Although I had photographed the Chesil bank many times, the shots never seemed to really capture the parabolic sweep of the beach curving towards the horizon. Recently, however, I spotted a band of cloud north of Dorchester moving to the south-west and my arrival on Portland Heights coincided with this image. The eyesore of the circular tanks, built on reclaimed tidal marshland, glistened in the sunlight after recent rain unlike Chiswell still lying in deep shadow in the foreground. The wind dropped and the decaying cumulo-nimbus beyond the fleet failed to produce any more interesting light.

Abbotsbury Hill

Equidistant between Weymouth and Bridport lies an Iron Age fort, and its inhabitants would have been the first Britons to appreciate this Dorset 'spectacular'. It was in the valley below that the chief steward of King Canute chose to found the Benedictine monastery, colonizing it with monks from Cerne Abbey. They probably didn't appreciate being sent to this rather secluded valley protected merely by Chapel Hill from the full force of the westerly gales. I prefer the site that the first Britons created astride Abbotsbury Hill, with its magnificent view along the sweeping curve of Chesil Bank to Portland on the horizon. How the planners once proposed to site a nuclear power station beside the Chesil in the middle of this photograph is beyond belief. Thankfully, they were dissuaded from doing so.

It's a steep climb up from the village of Abbotsbury to the fort, via its various roadside pull-ins and the ice-cream van in the small car-park at the top. I've always felt that the best photograph can be taken from half way up; at this point, where St Katherine's Chapel just breaks the horizon. The higher one climbs the more insignificant the chapel becomes. Although I set up my tripod at sunrise, the clouds, without which the shot wouldn't have existed, didn't appear until half an hour later. It proved to be the first and last frame for that day as it started to rain shortly afterwards.

Puncknowle Knoll

Standing quite alone on a hilltop between West Bexington and Puncknowle is a singularly odd 'one up one down' structure built on a Bronze Age barrow. The Lookout, as it is known locally, is thought to be 200 to 250 years old and beside it there was once a beacon which was lighted to announce the arrival of the French during the Napoleonic wars. It has a very dominating position with views stretching from Portland to Start Point in Devon. Some claim that the hill, and later the hut itself, were used by smugglers wanting to signal luggers carrying contraband. It is known that cargoes were often landed nearby and taken inland along the secluded country lanes, one of which is named after the famous smuggler, Isaac Gulliver. Others believe that the revenue men themselves used this vantage point to catch the smugglers. Whatever the Knoll's exact history there is no doubt that it is a superb spot from which to watch the sun set, the expanse of Lyme Bay mirroring the sky. A picture of the panorama from the Lookout would reveal little, however, and do no justice to the exhilarating feeling I derive from this spot; hence this stark shot of the building alone on the barrow.

Eggardon Hill

It is rumoured that on dark stormy nights one can still see the legionaries marching along the old Roman road leading to the fort on Eggardon Hill. I have never seen them, although the conditions have been perfect many times. The Romans were certainly not the first inhabitants, for the earthworks were originally erected in the Iron Age.

It is very bleak up here and cattle grazing on the windswept pastures have little shelter except in the lee of some of the fortifications. I had framed this shot up on the hill's southern flank several times, finally taking this photograph of the oblique sunlight illuminating the tops of the trees and the raised earthworks, which in fact enclose a 20-acre compound. Eggardon is a majestic fort. Although lower than Pilsdon Pen, the highest point in Dorset, and on the left of frame, it is more impressive with its awesome solidity.

Pilsdon Pen

Ordnance Survey now gives all heights in metres, but Pilsdon Pen – the highest point in Dorset – sounds much grander being described as 909 feet above sea level. Many of the forts of Dorset boast one of these triangulation points, any one of which must be in direct line of sight by at least two others. Their use is to satisfy the cartographer's need to view the world from on high. Often the position of these lumps of concrete means that their surroundings are bleak and open to all weathers, and Pilsdon Pen is no exception. The relative heights along the central Dorset ridge are very similar, with Bulbarrow only 7 feet lower, but I wanted to take my photograph here looking south across Marshwood Vale. On the horizon a sunbeam strikes the sea beyond Golden Cap, its outline invisible from the north. The Iron Age inhabitants of Pilsdon Pen enjoyed some of the best views in Dorset from this southern aspect; and from the northern side it is possible to see the Quantocks in Somerset.

Charmouth Beach in the Rain

This photograph was a race against time. A bank of dark cumulus clouds contrasting against the vivid blue sky was moving inexorably from the north-west towards the coast, after which the approaching sunset would be cloudless. Suddenly, as I was still formulating my plan for a photograph the heavens opened, the rain cutting through the strong evening sunlight (rainbow time). To show rain in a photograph it has to be backlit by the sun against a dark background. There was only one place where I thought I could achieve this, for in my mind I visualized looking west where the River Char meets the sea. Although I had estimated it to be only about a ten-minute drive, an A35 contraflow (red lights of course) and a dreaded caravan, hampered considerably.

In the beach car-park, the occupants of the other cars had their windows firmly closed against the heavy rain, as a mad photographer hauled his medium format gear out of the boot followed by a large tripod. No time for the brolly, it was buried too deep. Within two minutes I had exposed two frames with about thirty seconds between them; I felt like a contortionist with the cable release in one hand and the corner of my coat held over the camera with the other whilst balancing on tiptoe. As I looked up during the second exposure, the effect had vanished. The result exceeded my hopes.

Rampisham Bridge

Snug in the valley amid the chalk downland, towards Beaminster, is Rampisham, a very old and established little village which has hardly expanded at all. Many of those who visit do so because of the Tiger's Head, a fine inn. To them that is Rampisham, as the rest of it is concealed by tall trees down winding lanes. Through the heart of the village flows a small tributary of the Frome, though at this point in summer it had a pitiful amount of water in it. On previous occasions with the stream in full spate, I had formulated a shot of the other side of the bridge with a massive beech tree in the background, but the light had never been quite right. Then, during the stormy weather the beech blew down right across the lower part of the river-bed, its roots tearing the bank apart as it fell. My frame was ruined.

Returning several weeks later, I saw that the fallen tree had been removed and that the entire root system had been neatly severed and carefully placed back in the great hole that it had vacated, the river bank at that point safe from further erosion. I know nothing about the history of the little bridge, or why it is there. Being very narrow, it cannot be of tremendous use. Nevertheless I like it and took this frame in the evening light before the sun disappeared behind a hill on the edge of the village.

Long Barn at Abbotsbury

The largest larder in Dorset, the great barn at Abbotsbury has witnessed many turbulent happenings in its five hundred years or so of existence. It is a massive building, nearly a hundred yards in length. Unfortunately only about half the original structure remains intact. Surviving Henry VIII's Dissolution of the Monasteries and Cromwell's Parliamentary forces, the reed-thatched roof suffered severe damage during recent storms.

The barn has been photographed from almost every conceivable angle, but it was the detail of the stone walls in this case that fascinated me. I did not wish to photograph the barn, as is normally done, in its entirety. Added to this, the light had never before enthused me to get the cameras out of my case. But I changed my mind when I saw it just catching the buttresses in the late afternoon sunlight.

TARRANT RUSHTON AIRFIELD

In 1943 it was decided that there would be a change of use in the land surrounding Crooks Farm. Within days, the hedges and buildings had vanished; the airfield of Tarrant Rushton emerged several months later. Apart from becoming the hub of Second World War glider activity, it was the base for SOE (Special Operations Executive) covert operations into occupied Europe. The airfield was a small but essential cog in the vast war machine across southern England which was being assembled for the eventual invasion. Nowadays it is difficult to imagine the throng of aircraft, wingtip to wingtip, across the vast field. Long after the war the thresholds were specially strengthened to accommodate Vulcan bombers, but only one landed here. Eventually the airfield was pensioned off and the runway broken up to become the Wimborne bypass. To me, old abandoned airfields still have an aura about them and this particular monument encompasses much of its brief life. On a platform of the original runway are boulders from Portland and the Purbecks, together with pieces of the Pegasus bridge in Normandy and Salisbury Cathedral, once a homing point for returning aircraft. In the background lies the harvest; the land has returned to its original use but, alas, Crooks Farm is no more.

AIRBORNE
SOE
TO HONOUR ALL WHO SERVED
WITH 298 AND 644 SQUADRONS R.A.F.
C SQUADRON GLIDER PILOT REGIMENT

Minterne Magna from Little Minterne Hill

The Vale of Blackmoor was dank and overcast so I drove south up into the cloud-covered uplands, a day for exploration. It was the first time that I had visited Little Minterne Hill, part of the central Dorset watershed between the Frome and the Stour. Venturing along the unmetalled C road, the black shapes of tree trunks emerged out of the grey wind-borne mist: their tops were invisible. A slight drizzle began, making photography impossible in the monochromatic dawn. Further along, the ancient tree-shrouded earthworks of Dogbury enclosure at the end of the ridge had a very eerie quality.

After my slightly damp visit I left with a mental picture of what the area would look like in better light. I was unprepared for what I saw when I returned a month later: the landscape had been devastated by the storms. The trees on the enclosure were broken as if a massive foot had trodden in their midst, whilst many others along the ridge of Little Minterne Hill had succumbed totally. Amongst these, some, especially the pines, had been stripped naked of their branches, the debris being scattered between their not quite upright neighbours. I took this frame of a reptilian-shaped severed bough some months later during the summer. Looking down into the valley, Minterne House close to the source of the Cerne is partially obscured by the new foliage, the ravages of the previous winter's violent storms temporarily forgotten.

Milton Abbas

I find the existence of Milton Abbas village an enigma. Architecturally, the individual houses are boring in design, but collectively the myth of orderliness pervades and seen from the air it takes on the appearance of a vast excavation of some giant fossilized fish. The model village was not built for philanthropic reasons by Lord Milton but as a necessity to house the remaining inhabitants of the original town, which he had demolished in 1780. This was because he disliked having these neighbours so close to his great house built on the site of some tenth-century monastic buildings, which he had also destroyed. Many of the townsfolk were driven from the area for good and only those who worked his estate appear to have been provided with a new roof.

The incongruity of such a manicured village appeals, but what bothers me photographically is the inclusion of any cars for they ruin the simplicity of the gently curving street. However, by placing myself in the raised churchyard, I've created a different perspective, avoiding the problem. What the eye doesn't see, the brain need not imagine. Whilst composing the shot I was trying to work out how to make use of the shaft of light reflecting off a window behind me, when in the distance I heard the clip-clop of hooves. I had one chance at the frame as the pair of rather handsome nags provided the last component to the picture: their illuminated rumps.

St Luke's Chapel, Ashley Chase

Buried deep within some secluded woodlands on the edge of the Bride Valley lie the remains of a medieval chapel. I know the woods extremely well, as I used to play in them when young whilst staying at Ashley Chase. Despite that, it still surprises me when walking through them how the chapel suddenly looms ominously from the surrounding trees, the slate grey colour keeping it camouflaged to the last moment. There is no trace of any of the adjacent buildings that once stood here. The hamlet, being run by monks, was deserted after the Dissolution of the Monasteries in 1538. Nor is there any trace of a den a friend and I built nearby out of anything that came to hand. Our floor was made out of the forest marble exposed in the deep ravines surrounding the chapel. The rather odd shape of the sole surviving gable wall is due to some interesting restoration work, using the same source of forest marble, in the 1920s. In a bizarre way it adds to the character.

Stair Hole Strata

One can travel many hundreds of miles across some of the world's landmasses with the geology underfoot changing little in character, but the Dorset coastline makes up for any monotony elsewhere. The earth's surface is continuously moving, albeit very slowly. Newer chalk hills nearby are far less contorted than the older limestone Purbeck beds which stand almost vertically, showing clearly the last upper layers of the great Jurassic Age. The gentle folding of the chalk downs of southern England are a result of the ripple effect from the creation of the Alps, a young mountain range, which in turn exists due to the movement of the continental landmass of Africa. The older forces that disturbed the bands of rock in this 50-foot high cliff beside Stair Hole were much more severe. Looking like the rings of a tree, each of the bands in the rock may have taken thousands of years to create but every one tells a story of life at that time.

CERNE ABBAS GIANT

The history of Cerne Abbas itself is a lot more certain than that of its neighbouring giant cut into the chalk hillside. Some believe it to be a representation of Heracles dating from *c.* AD 187 but until the last century there was no mention of it in words or illustration. This may be because the figure was considered too indecent to record. The best way to see the Cerne Abbas Giant is en route from Yeovilton Air Station to Portland at 1,000 feet. Not being airborne, the standard view is from the trunk road ogling spot. However, I wanted to show the entire scene. The hillside figure in most colour shots looks flat, very much tied down by the two dimensional quality of a photograph, with the blue sky above the green hillside and little else. The Giant actually lies on the end of a long chalk spur, contrasting in my shot with hills beyond cast in total shadow. Waiting on the opposite side of the valley, it took ages for this particular configuration of light to occur. It only lasted ten seconds.

When one looks at the broader area one can see why the Giant was sited here as his symbolic fertility is clearly echoed in the shape of the hills to the north. Consult your Ordnance Survey map!

Fontmell Down

As far as I remember there was only one day of snow in Dorset at the beginning of last year, and that fell only on the upland areas, leaving a contour mark around the edge of the Vale of Blackmoor. Below, all was green. The weather front cleared to the south, leaving a crisp cold airstream blowing across the county, with small cumulus clouds forming briefly over the hills and then disappearing.

Fontmell Down is a finger of upland jutting into the eastern side of the Vale, 3 miles south of Shaftesbury and I was waiting nearby for the snow to stop falling. I freely admit that I'm one of those people who gets excited by fresh snow: if I'm not photographing the virginal landscape I would like to be tobogganing. On this day there was little time for the latter as it was already well past midday, leaving less than four hours of daylight; my planned itinerary ending up at Bulbarrow would require all that time. Excitement like this can sometimes get the better of me as I often prefer to ponder over a shot, watching the light change for some time before exposing a frame. Shooting rapidly and not methodically can lead to disappointment later in the darkroom. Not so the *contre-jour* effect here on Fontmell Down.

Breakwater at Lyme Regis

Lyme Regis has two separate centres, one based around the Cobb and the other to the east, where the main road crosses over the Lim as it enters Lyme Bay. The little river in its deep ravine is almost totally hidden by the surrounding buildings, as space is at a premium. At the bottom of the steep-sided valley the friable blue lias clay has been truncated by erosion of the sea. This erosion, which has always plagued Lyme, has resulted in a wide variety of walls to protect the town from Channel storms. The newer sea defences are by no means attractive, but they are more functional than the old one, whose broken remains lie on the sea-shore.

Almost everything in the photograph was fashioned or created by man – in the case of the Cobb on the horizon, several times. The Georgian houses which have been built virtually above the beach are beginning to suffer and unfortunately the more the sea threatens the properties, the uglier is the concrete response. The wonderful character of Lyme Regis has not as yet succumbed entirely to the twentieth-century onslaught: I hope it survives and does not become just another coastal theme park like Poole Quay.

Charmouth Bay with Golden Cap

According to many books this would have been an unwise place to be in AD 833, as thirty-five ships, full of rampaging Danes, were supposed to have disembarked on this shore to engage in what has been described as a 'great slaughter'. In fact King Egbert was not here doing his best to push them back to the beach, but was on the coast of Somerset. He did eventually re-establish the status quo.

Correcting this error wasn't the reason why I took the picture. It just happens to be one of the most beautiful parts of the Dorset coastline, with the Golden Cap as a backdrop. Usually, on a summer's day, there is a plethora of fossil hunters, whose patron Mary Anning (the finder of the fabulous ichthyosaurus) started a tradition of hacking away at the already eroding cliffs. Interestingly, one can trace these shale rock formations right across the country to Robin Hood's Bay in Yorkshire where other fossil hunters gather.

I prefer to wander the beaches and sift through likely patches of pebbles for a few ammonites amongst the abundant bits of broken belemnites, a squid-like creature. Jane Austen certainly would have sat near here when she described this as a 'sweet retired bay, beached by dark cliffs, where fragments of low rock among the sand make it the happiest spot for watching the flow of the tide'; the same tide that King Charles II failed to set sail upon when trying to flee from Charmouth.

HORTON TOWER

In the open countryside about 4 miles to the north of Wimborne is this 120-foot high folly, built nearly 250 years ago. The 6-storey brick tower perched on its low hill dominates the surrounding area. It certainly would not have obtained planning permission today. Horton Tower was originally described as an observatory, probably of a terrestrial nature as it was very useful for spotting deer.

The structure is totally hollow inside and it made an excellent setting for the cock fight in the film *Far from the Madding Crowd*. It was this image combined with the frequent visits I made when staying in the nearby village of Gaunt's Common that made me originally want to photograph its interior. Unfortunately barbed wire now stops all from entering and a sign warns of falling masonry: the structure is now sadly in decline. The countryside around is rather flat so I chose to shoot the tower silhouetted against an interesting sky. Such a sky occurred when the sun, shining through the alto status clouds, produced an uncommon spectral circular phenomenon. Positioning the camera in the shadow of the top of the tower enhanced the effect. All I then needed were some low level clouds to balance the composition; they were everywhere except where I wanted them. Whilst waiting for them to move into shot I had to reposition the camera several times as the lens emerged from the shadow of Horton Tower, simulating a massive sundial.

Seagulls above Durdle Door

One day the Durdle Door will succumb to the erosion of the pounding waves of the Channel storms. The isthmus of softer wealden clays will be washed away and the arch will collapse leaving only a stack of Purbeck rock as a reminder of its former grandeur. This too will soon be reduced to what we see in Man o' War bay, to the east of the promontory – a series of jagged rocky islets. The silhouette of this geological freak encloses the outline of a massive self-satisfied bird, and above, high up over the Door two seagulls rest, oblivious to their larger imaginary neighbour. I took this photograph on the shortest day of the year in 1981, the sea unusually calm for winter. Solitude is sometimes essential in such places in order to appreciate nature.

Durdle Door through the Arch

Some ten minutes after photographing the seagulls perched upon the narrow rocky ridge above Durdle Door I left the shingly beach, strewn with its flotsam and jetsam, tramped up the muddy steps held in position by wooden boards and emerged on the small plateau above. From this viewpoint I composed a shot using a long lens tight on the arch. Out of the several frames taken I chose the one in which the eddies and currents swirling around the base appeared to create the eye of a primeval bird. Its outline is formed by the silhouette of the formation itself. There are no half-tones to be seen, and the photograph has a peculiar lithographic quality.

Although the light was similar, this and the next shot have a very different feel, this one being the more introverted and abstract. The Durdle Door is one of the most famous features on the entire British coastline and I like Paul Nash's comment describing it as 'that well known eccentricity'. A similar label could also be attached to the people I know who take pleasure in abseiling from the top into the freezing water below, a dubious pastime, but the effect might have been very bizarre in my photograph.

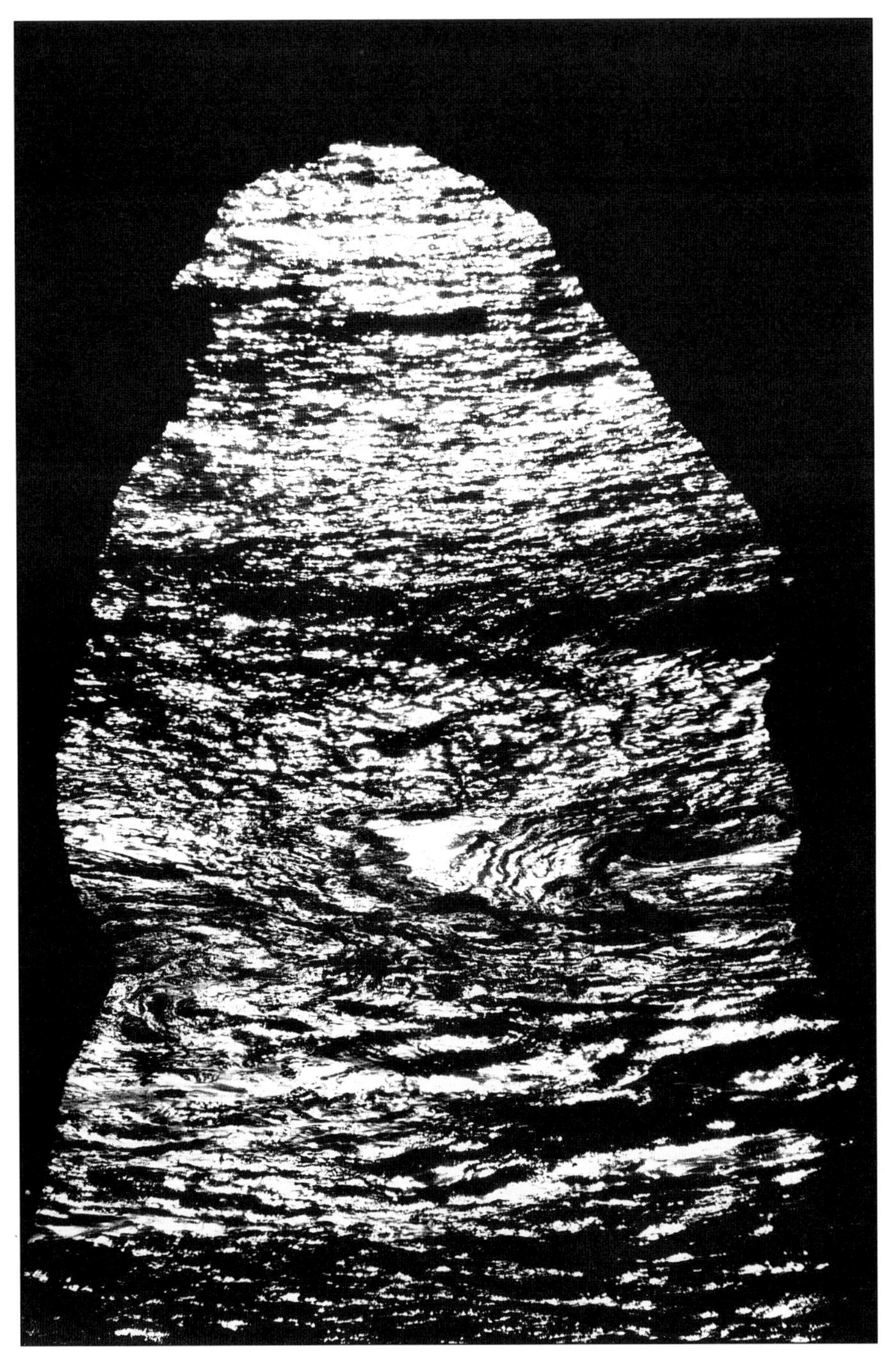

St Alban's Head

Inland there had been freezing fog overnight, but the Purbecks had escaped with only small amounts of mist accumulating in the valleys. Ascending Whiteways Hill from East Lulworth, the whole of the Frome Valley resembled a massive undulating off-white carpet obscuring every feature, broken merely by a near vertical plume of steam rising from the Winfrith nuclear power station somewhere below. Further in the distance, banks of heavy stratus clouds were forming, separated from the fog by a dark line. This delineated the central uplands of Dorset which resembled a distant coastline beyond the sea of grey. On reaching the top of Whiteways Hill I could see south into the Purbecks. As I erected the camera, I watched the remnants of the mists in the Tynham valley disappear in the last of the sunlight for that day. Although only early morning, an approaching front was already spreading a thin veil of cirrus overhead; soon it would obscure even the low winter sun. The visibility was fabulous, on the far promontory above St Alban's Head the buildings and chapel were clearly silhouetted against the bright horizon. There was a feeling of intense stillness over the Isle of Purbeck as new, ominous weather systems gathered in the skies above.

Penbury Knoll

Overlooking the barrows on Handley Down and Ackling Dyke is the most easterly of the Dorset hill forts, that of Penbury Knoll. The fort, now capped by conifers, surmounts a hill covered with extensive Celtic field systems. Looking for a shot I walked around the Iron Age fortifications, much of which have been destroyed by more recent gravel digging. I took several frames but none achieved what I had in mind. Rather than linger too long I left as the previously clear sky was changing. Low broken stratus below the very high cirrus clouds heralded the rather earlier than expected approach of the warm front. On the way back the shot I wanted appeared, with the Knoll in shadow suddenly taking on a sinister appearance beneath a now interesting sky, exaggerating the fort's dominance over the surrounding landscape. Beneath, clearly visible, are the dark lines of the Celtic fields surviving above the rectangular modern agriculture. The good light was short-lived, as two hours later the last vestiges of sunlight vanished for the day.

BOURNEMOUTH, FROM HENGISTBURY HEAD

Neither Bournemouth nor Christchurch were in Dorset until the major reshuffle in the county boundaries in 1972 when the Hampshire border receded. The transfer of the residents of this area to Dorset increased the county's population by a third. But such changes would have proved unnecessary had the area remained the deserted wilderness it was until Bournemouth's birth during the nineteenth century. Hengistbury Head and its very ancient heritage however, has remained intact, untouched by the urban sprawl. The bungalows of Southbourne stop short about half-a-mile from the Iron Age cross dykes, almost afraid to approach any closer.

Sitting amid the sparse vegetation on Hengistbury Head, I watched the sun slowly disappear into some distant clouds just above the horizon. The frame I wanted could only be taken after sunset at dusk, for the longer exposure then possible would give the sea in Poole a graceful texture and the lights on the promenade would have then begun to glow. Although a million people come here each year, I was on this Sunday evening in March quite alone. I did, however, since sunset, have the accompaniment of the sound of bells coming across Christchurch harbour from the priory two miles away.

Dancing Ledge

In cutting and removing the Purbeck stone into the coasters, the quarrymen created a perfect environment for the unloading of French brandy and other contraband which was taken up the steep smugglers' path to Spyway farm. Although not far from Swanage, Dancing Ledge has a wonderful isolation as you can only reach it on foot or possibly by boat (but only if it is reasonably calm). In rough weather the sea surges across the inundated rocky platform and at such times the smugglers must have thought the ledge an evil place to be.

The flora and scenery here has always reminded me of some stretch of rocky Mediterranean coastline and this includes its peculiarly unEnglish aroma. On this occasion when I arrived, there were several people scattered around so I chose my angle and sat patiently for about an hour; the sun's disappearance hastened their departure, leaving the two solitary fishermen who hadn't caught anything throughout my vigil. After taking the frames I wanted I moved to take several others on the ledge itself. Looking up to the cliff top I saw that my previous vantage point had been taken over by a seagull – I was obviously trespassing. It stared out impassively, perhaps just quietly waiting for the fishermen and myself to leave.

Nether Cerne

Hornblower once said that, 'the lucky man knows how much to leave to chance', and I try to abide by this axiom when out searching for frames, although there are times when it certainly isn't true. On one occasion I was driving south from Cerne Abbas to Dorchester when, casually glancing to my left, a convenient lay-by allowed me to stop. Behind me were the ingredients of a very good photograph. Before the mood changed I shot off three frames of colour on 35mm. There was no black and white photograph at that range, so I ran across the field to the river, and using it as a foreground took this shot. The horse obligingly had not moved too far in these few frantic moments and thankfully the last illuminating rays of the sun still bathed Nether Cerne. This odd little cluster of houses is dominated by the fifteenth-century tower, part of a much older church below.

Beside the Dorset Gap

Modern roads have left a small region right in the geographical heart of Dorset well alone. This area, straddling the central chalk ridge between Folly and Melcombe Bingham, has an isolated feel, but the activities of the past are much in evidence. In the centre where the ridge narrows, it appears that a great axe has cleaved a 'v' shape through the chalk, forming the Dorset Gap. This allows a north–south track to pass through at the bottom. Running parallel to the ridge are a series of earthworks of Iron Age origin, now much altered. Standing on one of these a few yards to the south of the Gap, I felt that I was looking upon one of the oldest roads in Dorset in the gully between two Iron Age embankments.

Maiden Castle

Maiden Castle is extraordinarily difficult to photograph and aerial shots generally do it the most justice. This is because the Iron Age hill fort is massive, the interior alone covers 47 acres. There was a bitter siege here in AD 44, after which the Romans stormed the then 400-year-old castle, and massacred most of the defending Britons. The simple but effective British sling-shot was in the end no match for the determined legions commanded by Vespasian.

I have wandered around its ramparts many times camera-in-hand and have rarely taken a photograph. Shots of any individual part of Maiden Castle are liable to be dull and boring as they fail to give an impression of its size and grandeur. Mood also is essential and for me is created by the shadows from a low sun, but often even this isn't enough to warrant a frame. Recently, however, sheep have been allowed to graze around the castle to help fix the grass on the inherently unstable banks. This instability had previously been exacerbated by cattle being allowed to roam freely across the castle and ramparts causing severe erosion to the fragile slopes. Repairing the scars of loose earth and chalk, which is quite a task, was undertaken by the Prince's Trust. If I hadn't seen this roll of sheep fence on top of one of the earthworks I probably wouldn't have included anything from Maiden Castle. The imagery is rather bizarre.

Rawsbury Camp in Winter

Joined by a narrow chalk spur to Bulbarrow is Rawsbury camp, the second highest Iron Age hill fort in Dorset. The fort's commanding central position overlooking such a vast area must have given it a particular importance. Certainly at a later date the Romans used it, leaving their coins and pottery as evidence. On this day, my arrival coincided with the last of the daylight reflecting off the temporarily snow-covered uplands. The Vale of Blackmoor to the north, bereft of any snow was quickly darkening with the onset of dusk. Besides enjoying the exhilarating air in the snowy landscape I decided to take a few frames, and before the sheep on the fort scattered, I took this one. A couple of seconds later even these two had disappeared leaving me with an empty horizon and the rather undefined entrance of this Iron Age fort.

Colmer's Hill, Symondsbury

I am certainly not the only person to have been intrigued by the conical shape of Colmer's Hill with its bunch of jaded pine trees on top. It is a 'natural' hill; its contours lie unchanged by Iron Age man, like much of the Dorset landscape. No listing appears for it amongst the archaeological records; this saddens me, as I've always felt that such a landmark *ought* to have some history.

The hill is not the easiest subject to photograph; from the new road to the south of Bridport it dominates your vision, but from the valleys below, one might never know of its existence as lofty trees obscure the summit. Choosing my position on the north side, off the road that leads to Marshwood Vale, I set up the camera only to have to wait for an hour as the cows slowly munched their way into shot. All I needed then was the right combination of cloud and shadow to create the picture. After several frustrating near misses finally the different elements of the composition came together. I only had a few seconds to take the shot, but it was enough.

Melbury Hill

Above Zig-Zag Hill on the border with Wiltshire is one of my weather assessment points. From my perch alongside the wood, I have seen the corn in the field growing, ripening and the naked stubble after the harvest. Up here I am able to judge the local variation of the clouds which control the nature of the light and from this decide on the possible tactics for the day's photography. Melbury Hill in the middle distance dominates this region of Dorset, overlooking both Shaftesbury to the north and the sweep of the Vale of Blackmoor to the west. It is a grand place. When I'm high up it's easier to see the shadow and light combinations and I can foresee a potential frame some minutes before it actually materializes; I waited twenty minutes for this one. I liked the idea of the harrow waiting in the foreground for the harvest and later its turn to be dragged across the field to prepare it for the following year.

The Cobb at Lyme Regis

'I fear for her safety' was the cry as the French lieutenant's woman was drenched yet again whilst perched on the end of the Cobb during a storm; as can been seen, quite rightly so. Being an artificial harbour the Cobb was a lot more successful in its task than Clavell's attempt at Kimmeridge and over the centuries a considerable amount of effort has gone into creating the harbour as it now exists. In the days of sail the coastline westwards from Portland Roads was very inhospitable and a wreck chart shows that even with the Cobb for shelter many vessels foundered in the vicinity; from the sea the Cobb appears very small and in a storm it must have required very exacting seamanship to gain the safety of its lee.

Lyme no longer relies on its harbour for its prosperity; this is now derived chiefly from the grockles who fill Lyme in summer and like to look at this fantastic edifice to man's success over the elements. I like to reserve my visits here to the shorter winter days when the winds are fresher and the Cobb is quieter; trying to photograph through people can be very frustrating especially using this, my favourite camera angle.

Weymouth Harbour

In my opinion, the recent sanitization of Weymouth Harbour was an ill-conceived idea. In a way it was inevitable after the pedestrianization of the town. As the most distinguishing landmark, the harbour had a character that had evolved slowly, repairs and alterations being done as necessary. To disregard all this by blanking out all those small features that look 'untidy' and kitsching the rest has for me broken the spell that the harbour once had.

I photographed it at night after imbibing at the King Charles. One of the advantages of a 30-second exposure is that people don't register on the film. It was a superbly calm evening; the movement in the fishing boats was infinitesimal and I feel that perhaps some of the old character still remains. Maybe in time things will look better, but the demand for such change should come from within and not be superimposed.

THE GEORGE INN
BEST BITTER
SEA COW
WH 43
WH 43

Tynham

Tynham is an evocative word for many. The displacement for the inhabitants of the village during the Second World War has yet to be reversed, as the army still control the whole of this area. The now deserted valley is cut off from the rest of Dorset by the great chalk escarpment on the northern edge of the Purbeck hills. Above this ridge, part of the geologist's paradise of the Isle of Purbeck, the black clouds gather for yet another heavy shower. Beyond the truncated valley forming Walbarrow Bay and the hazy sea is the slither of Portland on the horizon, the Isle's connection to the mainland appearing to be severed.

The car-park on Whiteways Hill is another of my weather watching points. Unfortunately access is only permitted by the Army when they open the ranges and I've been caught out a few times by forgetting what day of the week it is. However, the benefit of their presence is that it has prevented any development along this stretch of coastline. When the status quo is restored long may that remain so. Perhaps this could be a suitable excuse to allow the formation of a national park.

Ice-cliff at Kimmeridge Bay

The cliffs at the heart of Kimmeridge Bay on the Isle of Purbeck are dark grey and can have a very gloomy feel. At the base of these cliffs the beach has been totally obscured by vast heaps of decaying seaweed. The stench can be dreadful in summer. However, on this January day the landscape had been changed dramatically by an overnight blizzard. The ice-cold northerly wind was still blowing off the Purbeck hills, funnelling down across the bay when we arrived. The field car-park was empty, its white covering as yet untouched. No sun, just a flat, overcast snow-flurried sky. An ideal day for a walk, but not necessarily for photography. Armed only with a 35 mm lens on a Nikon the only frames I expected to take were those of my companions suffering from various degrees of frostbite. That was until I saw the ice-cliff. The underground water, which normally seeps out of the bituminous shale and dribbles down the grassy tufts, was being frozen into the most fantastic icicles. Despite the appalling light I like the shot and remember the day probably because the cups of tea later tasted so good.

Hartland Moor

There always seems to be an enormous desire in us either to contaminate or destroy any natural area. The vast tract of land, christened by Dorset's most celebrated writer 'Egdon Heath', has suffered considerably. At present there seems to be a three-pronged attack from the Army in the west, and the local planning office and the forestry commission elsewhere. The other little jewel in this crown – the nuclear research establishment at Winfrith – now appears to have sealed the fate of the heathland. A reference to Canford Heath normally refers to a modern urban sprawl, rather than what now lies beneath it, a sad state of affairs. The denigration of the heathland has continued since the Reformation, and some 70,000 tons of clay were removed annually from the Wareham area during the latter part of the last century. Thankfully nature has transformed the old clay pits into places of beauty.

Hartland moor, overlooked by Corfe Castle to the south, is one of the few surviving untouched areas, probably because it is only a few feet above sea level and rather marshy. Not a place for a walk, as the vegetation is very fragile, almost floating on its aqueous subsoil. The tree, a lonely specimen, stands totally out of place in its surroundings, an invitation for a photograph.

West Wood

Beyond West Wood and across the treeless Shepherd's Bottom the border with Wiltshire begins and claims much of the upland parts of Cranborne Chase. Sweeping into Dorset from the east, it is crowned with cross dykes and pitted with bottoms. The scarp slope with the old ox drove delineates the northern edge of the chase and a similar geographical feature, from where the Vale of Blackmoor extends, forms the western extremity. High above the vale are Fontmell and the aptly named West Wood.

It was here at West Wood, whilst driving past Compton Abbas airfield that I saw the low summer sun penetrating into the foliage. I wanted to achieve the idea of the dappled foliage and tree trunks floating in the dense blackness of the wood. The quiet evening was punctuated by the noise of the small Cessnas as they rotated skywards from the small airfield.

Up Cerne Church

The village of Up Cerne appears to have been stage-managed to give those who pass through it the maximum pleasure one can possibly derive from a tiny Dorset hamlet. Tucked away, it is obscured by the lie of the land from the main road running north from Cerne Abbas; passing traffic is totally unaware of its existence at the foot of an amphitheatre of chalk downland. The trees, which are an integral part of Up Cerne, fared much better than those on Little Minterne Hill nearby during the storms. It was with this aspect in mind that I wanted to formulate my shot.

Approaching from the main road with the lakes in a hollow to the left, I suddenly became enveloped by a shining canopy of beech trees which formed a shimmering avenue of light descending towards the hamlet. Through the leaves a shot encompassing the lakes seemed to be the most promising frame, but the composition didn't work properly, so I looked around, and behind the gently swaying limbs to one side I spotted the church. I feel that I have kept the seclusion of the hamlet intact in this rather unusual frame.

THE STOUR AT STURMINSTER MARSHALL

In May, the Frome is very shallow as it flows under the medieval eight-arched stone bridge at Sturminster Marshall. The tranquil scene belied the image I had witnessed the previous winter. Then, the silt-laden water had covered the entire area and had thrashed its way under the bridge. The reed banks had disappeared, leaving the bare trees vulnerable to the swirling currents. The architects who designed this structure created something that not only had massive strength but also harmonized totally with its surroundings. Rather than photograph the whole bridge, I found another spot on one of the massive buttresses jutting upstream, where the sun was making triangular shapes on the stonework. I wanted the lichen-covered stone to be dominant, its angles juxtaposed with the swaying trees on the riverbank. Keeping the foreground texture sharp was an interesting depth of field problem, but I calculated correctly. Looking at old photographs, I discovered that the summertime riverbank used to lie hard by the mill, with a road leading down into the river on the right. The building itself hasn't changed in the slightest.

Kington Magna

The northernmost part of Dorset centred around Gillingham has a separate identity to the south. Sandwiched between Somerset and Wiltshire, it has a rather featureless landscape except for a small escarpment overlooking the flat flood plains below. Whilst driving through Kington Magna, one of the villages on this slope, I glanced across at the cemetery of the Church of All Saints and saw this configuration of gravestones standing out against the sky. Although only 150 feet above the River Cale somewhere in the foreground, I could see Pilsdon Pen on the horizon which I placed between the 'v' of the gravestones; a familiar landmark even at this distance. The bisecting of the lines in the frame forms half the construction of the Star of David, an odd juxtaposition.

Freshwater Bay

More often than not the Bride, a diminutive river, fails to enter the sea normally as a rivermouth, instead it just seeps into the mass of shingle from a stagnant pool some yards inland. This pebble barrier part of the Chesil Beach is constantly remoulding itself across the mouth of the river. On this day the Bride was in spate, and as its valley is only 7 miles long the water quickly accumulates in the river after heavy rain. The rising level of the pool soon breaks over the top of the barrier in a wide flood narrowing down as it cuts a gorge for itself into the shingle bank.

Low stratus clouds were moving fast, just clearing the summit of Golden Cap in the distance; the ragged sea was now relatively docile compared with what it had been like a few hours earlier during the night. The caravans are a blot, but give the picture scale.

ACKLING DYKE

The modern Salisbury to Blandford road bisects the Bokerly Ditch on the Dorset and Hampshire border closely following and sometimes superimposed over the Roman road, until it finally diverges from its older counterpart, which continues south towards Badbury Rings in the form of Ackling Dyke. It is a fantastically well preserved piece of Roman engineering and is the most visible of all Roman roads in southern England. The open terrain on this edge of Dorset allows one to see the surviving earthworks scattered across the landscape; it is a remarkable area with an air of mystique.

The earliest man-made influence on this landscape took place in Neolithic times, and there is much conjecture as to the purpose, for instance, of the Dorset Cursus which runs roughly parallel with Ackling Dyke. Due to the relative flatness of this part of Cranborne Chase the 7-foot high agger of Ackling Dyke becomes a very prominent feature as it cuts across the wheat fields. A little further south a line of trees has been planted atop the Dyke, and I used these as a focal counterpoint to the cloud formation with the chalky speckle in the field stretching to the horizon.

Transposing the mood I feel for a particular area into a photograph requires patience and luck and this frame and another of the barrows on Handley Down a mile to the north (page 131) I took within thirty minutes of each other, following many previous abortive visits without a frame being exposed.

Huts on the Isle of Portland

On the leeward side of the raised beach on the southern end of Portland is a geometrical pattern of rocks and huts. Some of them are clearly used by fishermen, whilst others are much more secretive, their boarded windows obscuring all within. The one thing that they all have in common is that they all look different.

The salt air accelerates the deterioration of the paintwork causing it to craze and flake on the already uneven knotted wooden boards underneath; the resulting textural charm I find difficult to resist. I searched and found this hut with its side at an oblique angle to the sun, which accentuated this texture. All I had to do then was to hope that the right shaped cloud would appear in frame before the sun moved round too far. Because no cloud, no picture.

Rufus Castle above Weymouth Bay

Much of Rufus Castle no longer exists, as it has fallen into the cove below. When the castle was first built in Norman times it must have been a formidable place, almost a part of the rocky outcrop that formed its foundations. Today it has a very sad air, access is barred by a modern portcullis and visitors are definitely discouraged. Much of what remains was rebuilt at the end of the Middle Ages as a result of French excursions onto the Isle of Portland. Whatever state it is in now, the castle has been an integral part of the history of the island, and I wanted to try to capture its forgotten pride. Viewpoints are limited as on the seaward side the slope falls away steeply, so I selected this angle from the land side. It was late in the day and the heavy clouds overhead were obscuring the sun which was due to set in twenty-five minutes. Thankfully, the sun revealed itself five minutes before it set. The last light has just caught the corbels of the castle, contrasting with the dark cloud behind.

Perhaps Rufus Castle is beyond salvaging and it may be best to leave it alone on a perch high above the sea slowly to decay.

Blackmoor Vale, near Shaftesbury

The play of shafts of sunlight in between the racing shadows across open landscape can be fascinating; the whole mood and feel is constantly changing. Near Shaftesbury on the edge of the Vale of Blackmoor the terrain is gently undulating. It was here, after some gentle cruising around the area, that I stopped for the second time, the first having been for a police car which had seen me three times in different localities all near the Youth Detention Centre, Guy's Marsh. I muttered something about being a photographer in search of a landscape. Okeford Hill, on the horizon was visible through a shower brought here by the clear north-westerly airstream. Before this approaching shower was an amoeba-shaped 10-acre pool of light, moving to the left of the frame. Another area of light was cutting into the picture contrasting with the shower. Time for the shutter release.

Holway Hill near Sherborne

Cut off by Sherborne and the A30 is a small enclave protruding into Somerset. The whole character and feel of this 10-square-mile area is different from the rest of Dorset. I have tried to examine why, and my conclusions explain the reason for the photograph of Holway Hill. Immediately available evidence can be found by looking at older maps, for there have been two boundary changes: the first on 31 March 1896 when the villages of Sandford Orcas and Trent became part of Dorset and the second far more recently when Holway Hill followed suit.

Although not always as impressive as this, the stone belt of which the scarp slope of Holway Hill is part, can be traced via Castle Cary and Bruton to the Cotswolds. The limestone quarried in the area has resulted in a Somerset style of dwelling which contrasts for example with Milton Abbas in the chalk uplands. Finally, even the River Yeo which springs to life nearby on Poyntington Down deserts the county at Yeovil flowing to the north-west and the Bristol Channel. Holway Hill therefore typifies the allegiances found on this appendage to the county. Hence my frame looking to the north along the range of hills, with Cadbury Castle just visible under the broken bough.

Knowlton Church

It seems that speculation on the existence of the church within the prehistoric henge at Knowlton greatly exceeds any facts that are available. The remaining earthwork around the church is the only one left that is clearly visible. It has been a site of worship for four millenia up until the last century, when the little Norman church's roof finally gave in. Although the village it served was wiped out by the Black Death, its existence has nevertheless saved the henge from the same fate as its neighbours – the plough. However, by whom and why it was built, and the reason for siting the church in the middle is anybody's guess.

Even not knowing these answers, I, for one, can't help but feel that this is a special place, and despite the religious rites which may have taken place here it has a strange peace and attraction. Like many other ancient earthworks this neolithic henge is far more distinctive from the air but the resultant sterility can never convey the atmosphere of this tranquil place that seems to have taken revenge on the Christian intruder.

Bride Head, Valley of the Stones

Some special areas of the chalk uplands of southern Britain were once strewn with large boulders, scattered like massive grains of salt on a very large dinner plate. These hard conglomerate rocks were actually made and formed above the chalk but as the hard crusted material has cracked they have broken up. From Neolithic times the stones or 'sarsens' have been used as a convenient on-site building material for anything being constructed. The Valley of the Stones is one of the last areas where such boulders can be seen in one place; even relatively recently prints of Salisbury Plain show the ground covered with sarsens, but, together with many others, they have been removed by farmers. These stones are in the far upper reaches of the Bride Valley and it has often occurred to me that they resemble grazing cattle chewing the cud. Evidence of Stone Age activity appears on the far side of the valley in the low sunlight beyond the cows.

West Dorset

Beneath the heavy cloud the flat-topped hills of western Dorset sit squatly on the horizon with Golden Cap in the middle marking the northern encroachment of Lyme Bay. The farthest point, only just visible in the photograph, is Haytor on Dartmoor over 50 miles away; such visibility is rare. This vantage point is just to the south of Eggardon Hill on the road which curves along the ridge to the Spyway Inn in the valley below. The dreadful electricity pylons have also descended into this valley, though causing a lesser eyesore than their track across the tops of the downland to the north of the Bride Valley on the left of frame. Shortly after I took this shot, the banks of cloud increased and the rain fell, obliterating the sun's reflections on the green spring corn in the foreground. The power of the light was decreasing fast and by the time the clouds moved on, the shadows in the valleys had intensified. The time had come in this case to put the cameras away and to enjoy the intense blueness of the dusk sky, Haytor visible through binoculars to the last.

West Bay Storm

After a severe storm, around 4 million tons of shingle on the Chesil bank may be redistributed along its 18-mile length from here at West Bay to Chesil Cove underneath the tall cliffs on the Isle of Portland. Acting like a massive groyne, the shingle bank has protected the softer inland marl and clay from being eaten away by the ever-probing sea. There are many theories as to its existence, but I favour the idea that the pebbles originated from older coastlines to the south of the present one. As each headland eroded away the pebbles were allowed to accumulate, thus forming the Chesil Bank. One of my favourite places to view the fury of the sea is on the east jetty at West Bay. The man-made protrusion bisects the waves as they pass below to pound the beach with an explosive roar, followed by the muffled staccato of pebbles as the water recedes. At such times I've found that it is always best to keep half an eye out for extra large waves that threaten to dollop quantities of sea water over the camera – not such a good idea!

Poole Harbour and Round Island

Poole Harbour is a very fragile environment, and its beauty will soon disappear if taken for granted. Large sections of its 100-mile shoreline have been taken over by habitation, from Sandbanks right round to Holton point near Hamworthy. Agricultural methods have allowed greater amounts of topsoil to be borne down the Frome, causing the inland parts of the harbour to silt up faster than it should have done (Wareham was once a busy port). On top of all this there is the growing spectre of oil exploration.

I selected some tidal mud flats on the Arne peninsula avoiding the horrors elsewhere, for the southern part of Poole Harbour has generally been spared. From this low angle the Wych Channel this side of Round Island is invisible, just the white posts on the jetty can be seen above the water. The Purbecks straddle the horizon beyond the conifer plantations, which cover much of the heathland south of the harbour; in the foreground the rotted remains of something that once floated has become part of the silt, leaving the iron proud as a clue to its former use.

The Stag Gate, Charborough Park

Not far from the Stour at Sturminster Marshall is Charborough Park. This victory symbol of Sawbridge Erle Drax is barely seen as motorists overtake on one of the straight sections of the Wimborne to Bere Regis road. This was the first time I had stopped by the Stag Gate, on the edge of Charborough Park. The triumphal arch was erected when the road was re-routed around the Drax Estate. The incongruity of monuments like this often demands that they be photographed. I have succumbed many times to admiring the effects of folly-mania, when Englishmen who had large purses built edifices for posterity. However, I feel that Drax and the encumbant lineage that still reside in Charborough House have a reasonable excuse for wanting their privacy, as they have lived there since Elizabethan times. Who wants a main road through the front garden when it can be avoided? The Penny Black was a year old and photography had barely got its feet wet in 1841, when the arch and 2-mile perimeter wall were built along the road, excluding the motorist's prying eyes from seeing into one of the finest parks in Dorset.

Corfe Castle, Isle of Purbeck

As the focal point of the Isle of Purbeck, Corfe Castle is usually inundated with tourists, and their attendant coaches. I rarely stop here, and indeed usually avoid it altogether in summer. However I was lured by the personality of these great ruins, and wanted to achieve a picture with a different perspective.

The village of Corfe is just too picturesque to use as a foreground and besides, like almost all the villages of Dorset it is full of telephone wires. Other views through foliage and across fields have been exploited to their fullest extent – I've tried some of them in the past. All such photographs fail to encompass the feeling of what a formidable place the castle must have been to try and storm; they end up looking too pretty with no atmosphere. Many must have perished below the walls of King Edward I's present ruin; others would have been subjected to the ingenious medieval tortures of an earlier castle. I envisaged the photograph whilst waiting for the Wool level crossing gates to open: the moon's position gave me the idea. Would I be able to reach Corfe before sunset? Without the last of the sunlight touching the top of the battlements the frame would probably fail. The rest, like the castle, is history.

Gerrard's Hill, Near Beaminster

Buried in the middle of this photograph is Beaminster, camouflaged in the shadow amongst numerous trees. An hour earlier the scene had been entirely different as a thick layer of stratus cloud was holding down a blanket of haze, with the outline of the distant Gerrard's Hill barely visible. It was a miserable day for photography; the forecast had not predicted the flat light I was having to endure. It was the same everywhere so I left the car and wandered down a track to a field of rape in full flower. Emerging at the edge of the field I looked back across the valley, only to see the bank of clouds clearing to the south taking the haze with it. Returning along the track I prayed the light would hold as further clouds began to build up. I need not have hurried; I had at least half an hour to expose several frames from which I chose this one.

The Frome at Grey's Bridge

Late one summer's evening as I was crossing Grey's Bridge on the eastern edge of Dorchester, when I thought I had taken my last shot of the day as the light was fading rapidly, out of the corner of my eye I saw this reflection of the sky in the Frome. Three minutes later saw me clambering around on the bank of the river composing this frame. No detail would remain in the trees or the meadow when I exposed for the highlights. Even so it was quite a long exposure allowing the water in the foreground to show movement, but the still air moved neither trees or reeds.

The river and its flood plain have prevented the expansion of Dorchester to the north and here at Grey's Bridge it is much quieter now that the by-pass has not only removed the traffic but has also encapsulated the town's southern extremities. None of this would have bothered the Romans whose original bridge would have stood on this exact site.

Handley Down Barrows

I wanted a photograph of a barrow. The parish of Winterborne St Martin (Martinstown) contains more barrows than any other in Dorset – 118 to be exact so it came as a surprise to me that my barrow photograph came from the area of Handley Down, near Sixpenny Handley. To me, barrows create a stepping stone from the earth to the sky and their sites on hilltops and ridges reinforce this. For those buried in the barrows, it was the life to come, and not the life past that was important. By placing the barrow into near silhouette beneath a mystic sky, I have tried to echo visually the beliefs of Iron Age man. All this was done with my feet planted firmly in one of the ditches beside Ackling Dyke.

Winterbourne Came

I can't say that when I took this photograph these words of William Barnes, who lived at Came House, came to mind:

> The evening, gliding slowly by,
> Seems one of those that long have fled;
> The night comes on to star the sky
> and then it darkened round my head.

But looking at the print later this extract from his *Musings*, written late in his life, seemed to fit. Barnes, it appears, had the ability to do almost everything exceptionally well. It was perhaps the rejection by London theatres of his early plays that was the making of his poetry. Even though Came House and the fifteenth-century church, where William Barnes is buried, is less than a mile from Dorchester, it remains an enchantingly isolated little valley.

I do not understand why Francis Cartwright who designed Came House decided that it should be built on a north-facing slope, but despite this it is certainly an eighteenth-century masterpiece.

The Portland stone facing of the house was reflecting the last glow of the evening sky. This balanced the brightness of the moon and was a photographic opportunity not to be missed.

MARSHWOOD VALE

Within the western promontory of the county is Marshwood Vale, still a secretive place like the Bride Valley once was. Part of the fascination of the vale is its geology. Enclosed by some of the highest ground in Dorset to the north and the coastal hills to the south, it is in fact an eroded dome of different rocks. The gently dipping edges of the pericline are visible on the top of Pilsdon Pen. When I like the landscape of an area, I always try to understand its geology. Such is the case with Marshwood Vale.

In a strong blustery wind I had been photographing the showers as they sped eastwards, the patches of sunlight riding a switchback across the vale's rolling featureless margins. During one of these moments I took this frame, the trees stark against the momentary brilliance of the rain-sodden fields.

Walbarrow Tout

This part of the Dorset coastline is not always open to the public as it is controlled by the Army. Walking along the path on top of Whiteway Hill leading to Flowers Barrow Fort laden with camera gear, I kept on thinking that I had dropped a lens shade, as metal clanked against the flint. Looking down, all I had done was to kick yet another rusty and contorted piece of shrapnel – proving that this was a very live firing range. Tynham valley protected by its mini Rock of Gibraltar, the Tout, at the seaward end has the legacy of the abandonment. There is an eerie feel to the area similar to that when villages are revealed by lowering reservoirs during the summer droughts.

Having arrived at the fort I was so preoccupied with photographing Arish Mel that I only just managed to check behind me in time. A ray of sunlight had dramatically illuminated Walbarrow Tout, lifting it from its darker surroundings. The last time I had tried to photograph the Tout it had been a failure because of vibration from the wind. I would have failed again had I not glanced over my shoulder. The promontory itself is composed of the same Purbeck beds which reappear from the sea to the west as the Mupe Rocks, making the Walbarrow Bay a very much enlarged Lulworth Cove. This reciprocal shot to the first in the book, which I took from the isolated fort shows that nature is a certainly a superb sculptor. A fitting end to my photographic foray around Dorsetshire.

PHOTOGRAPHIC ANALYSIS

Some may argue that it is permissible to create a landscape print using several different negatives. I do not hold to this belief: all the images in this book were made from single frames. Also, I believe reversing frames of any particular scene, to enhance the composition, is a misrepresentation of actuality. Within the confines of a single negative, however, the role of the photographer/printer is analogous to that of a conductor working with a score, as the performance or print is a very personal interpretation of the base material.

I rarely use a 35 mm camera for black and white landscape and only when larger format cameras are not to hand. However when relying on 35 mm I like to use a 1936 Leica III A. I find the older uncoated Summar lenses are less contrasty, allowing greater detail to be obtained in the shadow areas. As my range of lenses for the Leica is limited, I also use Nikon FE 2s. For medium format, although I like the Mamiya RB 67 with its wider proportions, it is too bulky to carry far. The majority of the photographs have therefore been shot on a well-used Hasselblad CM which I'm able to tuck easily into one of the pouches slung around around my waist, when walking any distance. However, I think the ultimate quality comes from using 5 x 4 but it is often too slow to set up, besides which my Horseman is extremely heavy. The only images shot on 5 x 4 were St Alban's Head and the sunrise from Abbotsbury Hill. In general I prefer manual cameras as I hate having to rely on batteries and electrical innards to make them work, and this includes my Weston light meter (a selenium cell does not require batteries). The wiggly-amps tend not to wiggle so much after I've dragged them over ditches and across several fields.

The 25a wratten (red) filter, which I sometimes resort to is a bit like a sledge-hammer. More often, for subtler skies, I prefer what used to be known as a 'salmon' filter, equating to a weak wratten 85, losing only 2/3 of a stop. Because of the slow film and the occasional heavy filters that I use, I'm never without my tripod. I always have several in the car of differing weights, and am guided by the premise that the further I have to walk the lighter the tripod I carry.

The film I tend to use mostly is Agfapan 25 120, processed in Agfa chemicals. This gives a virtually grainless image compared to some of the earlier 35 mm frames using Ilford FP4, such as the photograph of Freshwater Bay. All of the prints have been made on my old Prefect enlarger using Oriental Seagull processed in Agfa 'Neutol' WA or BL. The glossy surface and very white base of this bromo-chloride fibre paper suits my imagery most of the time.

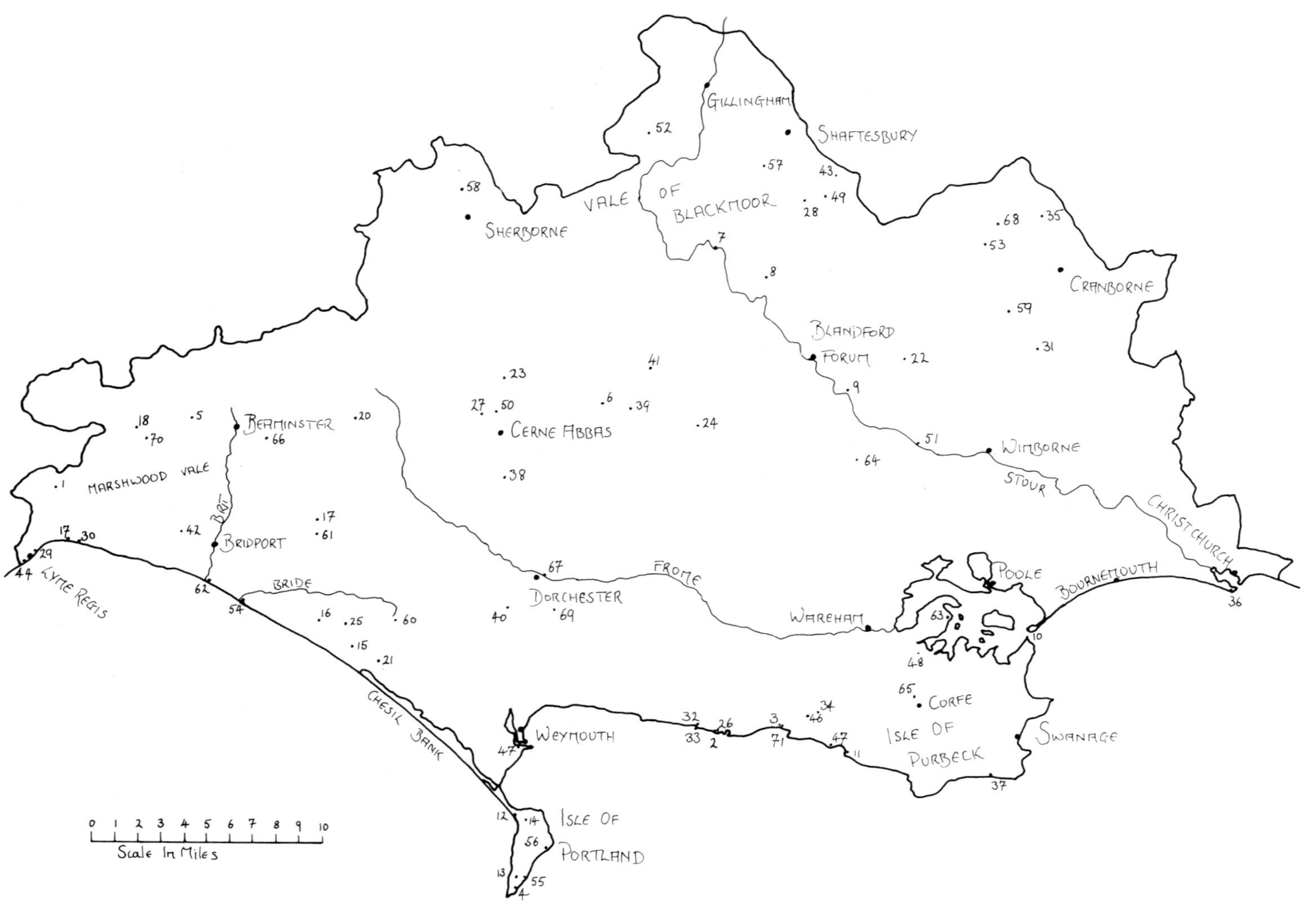

GILLINGHAM
SHAFTESBURY
SHERBORNE
VALE OF BLACKMOOR
CRANBORNE
BLANDFORD FORUM
CERNE ABBAS
BEAMINSTER
MARSHWOOD VALE
BRIT
BRIDPORT
WIMBORNE
STOUR
CHRISTCHURCH
FROME
DORCHESTER
BRIDE
LYME REGIS
POOLE
BOURNEMOUTH
WAREHAM
CORFE
ISLE OF PURBECK
SWANAGE
WEYMOUTH
CHESIL BANK
ISLE OF PORTLAND
0 1 2 3 4 5 6 7 8 9 10
Scale In Miles

TECHNICAL DATA

MAP NO.	TITLE	CAMERA	LENS	SPEED	STOP	FILTER
1	CONEY'S CASTLE TO CHARMOUTH	H'BLAD CM	50 MM	1 SEC	F22	SAL
2	BESIDE STAIR HOLE	H'BLAD C	50 MM	2 SECS	F16	NONE
3	MUPE ROCKS AND PORTLAND	H'BLAD CM	50 MM	1/15	F22	SAL
4	DERRICK ON PORTLAND BILL	HASELBLAD	50 MM	1/60	F16	15
5	LEWESDON HILL AND PILSDON PEN	MAMIYA RB 67	127 MM	1/8	F16	NONE
6	NETTLECOMBE TOUT	H'BLAD CM	40 MM	1/4	F22	15
7	STOUR NEAR HAMMOON	H'BLAD CM	80 MM	8 SECS	F16	NONE
8	IWERNE FROM HAMBLEDON HILL	H'BLAD CM	50 MM	1/4	F22	11
9	STOUR AT CHARLTON MARSHALL	MAMIYA RB 67	127 MM	1/8	F22	NONE
10	THE HAVEN, SANDBANKS	H'BLAD CM	50 MM	1/15	F22	15
11	KIMMERIDGE, CLAVELL'S PIER	MAMIYA RB 67	50 MM	6 SECS	F32	NONE
12	CHISWELL BOATS	H'BLAD CM	40 MM	1/8	F22	NONE
13	LIGHTHOUSES, PORTLAND BILL	H'BLAD C	100 MM	1/2	F16	25
14	CHESIL BANK	H'BLAD CM	50 MM	1/8	F11	SAL
15	ABBOTSBURY HILL	MPP 5 × 4 PRESS	8 IN EKTAR	1/5	F16	25
16	PUNCKNOWLE KNOLL	H'BLAD CM	40 MM	1 SEC	F16	25
17	EGGARDON HILL	MAMIYA 67	50 MM	1/4	F22	SAL
18	PILSDON PEN	H'BLAD CM	50 MM	1 SEC	F22	11
19	CHARMOUTH BEACH IN RAIN	MAMIYA	50 MM	1/30	F11	21
20	RAMPISHAM BRIDGE	H'BLAD CM	50 MM	1/2	F22	NONE
21	LONG BARN AT ABBOTSBURY	H'BLAD CM	40 MM	1/2	F22	NONE
22	TARRANT RUSHTON AIRFIELD	H'BLAD CM	40 MM	1/4	F22	SAL
23	MINTERNE MAGNA FROM LITTLE MINTERNE HILL	H'BLAD CM	50 MM	1 SEC	F22	NONE
24	MILTON ABBAS	H'BLAD CM	50 MM	1/15	F22	NONE
25	ST LUKE'S CHAPEL, ASHLEY CHASE	H'BLAD CM	40 MM	2 SECS	F22	11
26	STAIR HOLE STRATA	H'BLAD CM	50 MM	4 SECS	F22	25
27	CERNE ABBAS GIANT	MAMIYA RB 67	127 MM	1/8	F16	SAL
28	FONTMELL DOWN	MAMIYA RB 67	50 MM	1/15	F16	11
29	BREAKWATER, LYME REGIS	H'BLAD CM	80 MM	1/2	F16	NONE
30	CHARMOUTH BAY WITH GOLDEN CAP	MAMIYA RB 67	127 MM	1/2	F11	25
31	HORTON TOWER	H'BLAD CM	50 MM	1/4	F8	25

MAP NO.	TITLE	CAMERA	LENS	SPEED	STOP	FILTER
32	SEAGULLS ABOVE DURDLE DOOR	LEICA 111A	5 CM S'MAR	1/60	F9	NONE
33	DURDLE DOOR THROUGH THE ARCH	LEICA 111A	9 CM ELMAR	1/200	F12.5	NONE
34	ST ALBAN'S HEAD	HORSEMAN 5X4	300 MM	4 SECS	F32	21
35	PENBURY KNOLL	H'BLAD CM	50 MM	1/8	F11	SAL
36	BOURNEMOUTH, HENGISTBURY HEAD	H'BLAD CM	80 MM	4 SECS	F16	15
37	DANCING LEDGE	H'BLAD CM	80 MM	2 SECS	F22	NONE
38	NETHER CERNE	H'BLAD CM	50 MM	1/8	F16	NONE
39	BESIDE THE DORSET GAP	H'BLAD CM	50 MM	1/15	F16	SAL
40	MAIDEN CASTLE	H'BLAD CM	40 MM	1/8	F22	SAL
41	RAWSBURY CAMP IN WINTER	H'BLAD CM	80 MM	1/15	F11	11
42	COLMER'S HILL, SYMONDSBURY	MAMIYA RB 67	127 MM	1/4	F11	25
43	MELBURY HILL	H'BLAD CM	50 MM	1/4	F22	SAL
44	THE COBB AT LYME REGIS	H'BLAD C	50 MM	4 SECS	F22	NONE
45	WEYMOUTH HARBOUR	H'BLAD CM	50 MM	30 SECS	F22	NONE
46	TYNHAM	H'BLAD CM	80 MM	1/4	F11	SAL
47	ICE-CLIFF AT KIMMERIDGE	NIKON FE2	35 MM	1/15	F8	NONE
48	HARTLAND MOOR	H'BLAD CM	50 MM	1 SEC	F22	15
49	WEST WOOD	MAMIYA RB 67	50 MM	1/2	F22	NONE
50	UP CERNE CHURCH	MAMIYA RB 67	50 MM	1/2	F22	NONE
51	STOUR AT STURMINSTER MARSHALL	H'BLAD CM	40 MM	2 SECS	F22	21
52	KINGTON MAGNA	H'BLAD CM	50 MM	1/2	F22	NONE
53	FRESHWATER BAY	LEICA 111A	5CM S'MAR	1/40	F6.3	NONE
54	ACKLING DYKE	H'BLAD CM	50 MM	1/2	F16	SAL
55	HUTS ON THE ISLE OF PORTLAND	H'BLAD CM	40 MM	2 SECS	F22	25
56	RUFUS CASTLE ABOVE WEYMOUTH BAY	H'BLAD CM	50 MM	1/2	F11	SAL
57	BLACKMOOR VALE, NEAR SHAFTESBURY	MAMIYA RB 67	50 MM	1/2	F11	21
58	HOLWAY HILL NEAR SHERBOURNE	H'BLAD CM	50 MM	1/4	F22	15
59	KNOWLTON CHURCH	H'BLAD C	50 MM	1 SEC	F11	15
60	BRIDE HEAD, VALLEY OF THE STONES	MAMIYA RB 67	127 MM	1/2	F16	11
61	WEST DORSET	MAMIYA RB 67	127 MM	1 SEC	F11	15
62	WEST BAY STORM	H'BLAD C	80 MM	1/4	F11	NONE
63	POOLE HARBOUR AND ROUND ISLAND	H'BLAD CM	50 MM	1 SEC	F22	SAL
64	THE STAG GATE, CHARBOROUGH PARK	H'BLAD CM	50 MM	2 SECS	F16	25
65	CORFE CASTLE, ISLE OF PURBECK	H'BLAD CM	50 MM	6 SECS	F16	15
66	GERRARD'S HILL, NEAR BEAMINSTER	MAMIYA RB 67	127 MM	1/2	F16	POLA
67	THE FROME AT GREY'S BRIDGE	MAMIYA RB 67	50 MM	4 SECS	F16	NONE
68	HANDLEY DOWN BARROWS	H'BLAD CM	40 MM	1/4	F16	SAL
69	WINTERBOURNE CAME	MAMIYA RB 67	50 MM	6 SECS	F11	29
70	MARSHWOOD VALE	MAMIYA RB 67	50 MM	1 SEC	F22	SAL
71	WALBARROW TOUT	H'BLAD CM	50 MM	1/4	F16	SAL

PHOTOGRAPHERS' BRITAIN